How To Become A Dental Leader

By

Ike H. Rahimi, DMD

Table of Contents

About the Second Edition 9

Chapter 1: Introduction 11
   A. Lack of Leadership in My Earlier Days 12
   B. Your Team 13
   D. Time to Grow into a Stronger Person 16
   E. What's to Come 17

Chapter 2: Leadership 20
   Learning Objectives 21
   A. The Need for Leadership: Why Becoming a Leader is Key to your Success 21
   B. There is more than One Leadership Styles 24
   C. Discovering Your Leadership Style 26
   1. Self-Assessment 27
   2. Feedback from Others 28
   3. Identifying Areas for Improvement: The Why Must Be Answered 28
   4. Education and Training 30
   5. Seeking Mentorship and Coaching 32
   D. Adapting Your Unique Leadership Style 33
   E. Continuous Evaluation of your Leadership 34
   F. Putting Words into Action 35
   G. Put Your Team First 37
   H. Know Your Team Members 41
   Summary 44

Chapter 3: Office Vision 46
   Learning Objectives 47

A. Planning Equals Vision..48
B. Your Vision: A Guiding Light for Others 50
C. Creating a Vision and a Vision Statement..................51
D. Key Components of an Office Vision 53
E. Some Examples of Vision Statements........................55
F. Implementing the Vision 55
G. Money and It's Affects in the Office 58
H. Work Family..59
I. Nothing Stays the Same 60
Summary...62

Chapter 4: Becoming a Great Communicator........... 64
Learning Objectives..65
A. Why Being a Great Communicator is Key to Leadership..65
B. How to Become an Effective Communicator..........67
C. Steps in Actively Listening to People 69
D. Body Language 71
E. Feedback 72
F. Consistency 73
Summary...74

Chapter 5: Creating a Team.. 76
Learning Objectives..77
A. My Learning Mistakes...77
B. The Team Will Watch Your Back 78
C. Building a Great Dental Team: A Concise Guide ..80
2. Train Effectively 82
3. Foster a Positive Culture 82
4. Communicate Openly...83
5. Motivate and Reward 84

    D. Identify and Focus on Each Person's Skills and Potential..86
    E. Guiding Towards Self-Improvement 86
    F. Stop Micromanagement 87
    Summary...88

Chapter 6: More Freedom: The Power of Delegation 89
    Learning Objectives...90
    A. Take Charge..90
    B. Some Tasks Cannot Be Delegated 91
    C. Stay Calm Because Your Team Notices...................93
    D. More Free Time..94
    E. The Process of Delegation..95
    F. Failures and Setbacks...97
    G. Pick the Right Person for the Task 98
    Summary...100

Chapter 7: How to Make Changes in the Office 101
    Learning Objectives...102
    A. The Need for Change 102
    B. Steps for Successful Change....................................104
    C. Other Matters to Keep in Mind..............................109
    Summary...112

Chapter 8: Summary 113

About the Second Edition

The first edition of this book was written in 2015 and subsequently published in 2017. Reflecting upon the dental industry's evolution since that time, numerous transformations have materialized. Firstly, the Covid pandemic ushered in lasting changes. Secondly, dentists face greater challenges in recruiting exceptional employees. Thirdly, insurance companies have reduced their reimbursements. Fourth, there are more and more safety regulations that must be put in place.

Experiencing situations like losing half of your employees, receiving advice to close your office for 3 months, and only see emergency patients has affect the dental industry. These kinds of encounters have the power to change a person profoundly.

Through all the challenges of the Covid pandemic, the new ways of practicing dentistry, and much more, I gained new perspectives on how to lead a dental team.

It was finally time to embark on the journey of rewriting this book on dental leadership, infusing it with fresh and captivating content. I hope you enjoy reading this book as much as I enjoyed writing it.

CHAPTER 1:

Introduction

> *"To be successful, you have to have your heart in your business, and your business in your heart."* - Thomas Watson, Sr., former CEO of IBM.

I wrote this book with one primary intention: to share my two-decade-long journey of navigating the challenging waters of leadership within the context of a dental office.

The dental school curriculum equipped us with the basic clinical skills, but the vital element of leadership was noticeably absent. When I took the plunge and bought my first office, I was excited yet naive, not realizing that dentistry was not just about perfecting smiles but also about leading a team.

A. Lack of Leadership in My Earlier Days

The initial years of owning an office were marred by countless mistakes resulting from a lack of refined leadership skills. The office environment was often tense, affecting both the staff's morale and the patients' satisfaction. My lack of experience in leading and managing a team was manifesting as heartache in my office, hindering the growth and success I had envisioned.

During a particularly turbulent two-year period, my lack of leadership skills became glaringly apparent, as I found myself grappling with a high turnover rate. This revolving door of staff not only disrupted the office environment, but it also strained relationships with patients who had come to appreciate familiar faces.

One of the biggest challenges I faced was the art of hiring the right people. I found myself at a loss, unable to distinguish between a good fit for my office versus a potential liability. I often ended up hiring individuals who were impressive on paper but lacked the necessary interpersonal skills. They could not work with others in a team setting, they wanted to be the alpha employee bossing others around and they were always right.

They were recently hired and their cup was already full, how can someone like this learn new things?

Clinical skills could indeed be taught, but they were merely a fraction of the equation. The true essence of success in any field lies in the combination of those teachable skills with the right attitude and ingrained work ethics. These intrinsic qualities, nurtured over time, become the pillars upon which one's professional growth is built, propelling individuals to reach new heights of excellence.

Furthermore, I did not have an efficient training system in place for my team. I had assumed that hiring individuals with the right qualifications would suffice, but I soon realized that their success in my office was largely dependent on the level of training and guidance I provided.

B. YOUR TEAM

Just because an employee has prior experience working in another office doesn't mean they are already equipped with the necessary skills and knowledge for your specific environment. Remember, standards vary greatly from one dental office to another. The way they conduct procedures, manage patient relations, or even maintain the office cleanliness and organization could be drastically different from your expectations. Leadership involves recognizing these differences and providing the necessary training and guidance to align your team with your office's standards. Never assume and always verify, shaping your team members according to the vision, values, and standards that define your dental office.

It can be quite surprising and even disheartening to find that some offices still resemble stepping into a time machine. These archaic workplaces stubbornly cling to outdated methods, failing to capitalize on the countless possibilities offered by modern technology. As a result, employees who transition from such offices into a modern work environment must undergo a significant reorientation and be educated about the latest trends, tools, and practices that shape the modern workplace. We must bridge this knowledge gap and help them adapt to the modern ways of doing things, ensuring their smooth integration into the dynamic and fast-paced world of contemporary offices.

C. Knowing How to Handle Complex Dental Cases

Handling complex dental cases was another challenge that I encountered during my career. These cases often presented unique and intricate dental issues that required a higher degree of technical skill and experience to address effectively. As a dentist, I understood the importance of being adequately prepared for such cases, as they could quickly become overwhelming without the appropriate knowledge and expertise.

In my pursuit of providing exceptional dental care, I also made a conscious decision to lower my fees for these cases. I wanted to ensure that cost would not be a barrier for patients seeking the specialized treatment they needed. By reducing my fees, I aimed to make quality dental care more accessible and affordable for those requiring complex dental procedures.

Despite my best efforts, there were instances when certain cases did not turn out as expected. In such situations, I took full responsibility for the outcomes and refunded the fees to those patients or fixed it several times at no cost to the patient. It was essential for me to prioritize patient satisfaction and ensure that they received the best possible care, even if it meant adjusting the financial aspect of the treatment.

I recall a particular case in which a patient presented with a broken upper denture. The absence of the hard palate region on the acrylic denture resulted in the area resembling a horseshoe shape. The denture was fractured in the midline between the central incisors.

During our discussion, I explained to the patient that without the palatal seal, the denture would not stay securely in place. However, despite my recommendation, she insisted on proceeding without it due to her significant gag reflex. Although implants were a viable option, she declined.

Determined to find a solution, I dedicated considerable effort to crafting another horseshoe-shaped denture. Unfortunately, it did not work because as soon as the denture was inserted in the mouth, it fell out because it did not have a suction to hold it in place. No palatal seal equaled no suction and thus no retention. As a result, I refunded the patient's payment. This experience served as a valuable lesson.

When we issue a refund to the patient, we actually refund double the amount. Allow me to explain using this particular example. This patient visited us on 4-5 occasions for the creation of their denture, consuming 1 hours of chair time at each visit. Additionally, we incurred lab costs and significant time invested by our staff. When we refunded the patient's money, it was impossible to recover the lost chair time, lab expenses, and employee hours.

It is common for dental leaders to focus so much on the management and operational aspects of running their practice that the clinical side begins to slip. When faced with complex cases, the shortcomings in clinical knowledge and practice can become glaringly apparent.

D. TIME TO GROW INTO A STRONGER PERSON

Every challenge is an opportunity for growth. My experiences, both the triumphs and the failures, turned into important life lessons. Over the years, I learned to evolve my leadership style, to delegate effectively, to manage conflicts, and to steer my team towards a shared vision. I grew to understand people and to use that knowledge to determine which cases to accept and which ones to refer out.

My experiences will serve as a useful guide for others navigating the same path. Leadership is not just a title. It is a responsibility, a skill that can make or break your business. This book will help you reduce the pitfalls of running a dental office. I said reduce and not avoid because even with the best laid out plan, there will be challenges that await you. Life without obstacles and especially a business without issues is impossible, but as long as we are prepared for it as best as possible, then we are on a great path to thrive.

E. What's to Come

This book is about leadership, a subject that will be covered in detail, yet there are other components of being a great leader.

Office vision is the guiding light, a clear depiction of what you aspire for your dental office to be. The vision is what you want your practice to look like in terms of patient care, team harmony, profitability, services offered, and reputation in the community. It reflects the values and principles that underline your practice.

From that, we move on to becoming a great communicator. Effective communication creates a bridge between differing viewpoints, fostering an environment of understanding and cooperation. It helps in conveying your vision to your team, enabling them to understand their individual roles and how they contribute to achieving the office's overarching goals. It empowers you to handle conflicts and challenges proactively so that you can solve disputes and maintain a harmonious work environment.

No dental office is successful without a stellar team. It is the backbone of any successful business. They are the individuals who interact with patients, provide care, and ensure the smooth operation of the office. They uphold the office's reputation, foster strong relationships with patients, and contribute to a thriving practice.

Delegation is a fundamental aspect of leading a successful dental office. You can't, and shouldn't, do everything yourself.

Delegating tasks creates room for you to focus on high-value activities that require your expertise and attention. It's about entrusting tasks to your capable team, thus fostering a sense of responsibility and ownership among them.

Let's face it, most people don't like change, but it is essential to bring about change in a dental office to stay competitive and provide superior patient care. Implementing change, however, must be done in a structured and thoughtful way to ensure success.

With the groundwork laid out, it's time to roll up our sleeves and get to work. Leadership in a dental office is a journey, not a destination. As we delve deeper into the facets of leadership, we'll explore how to nurture a culture of excellence, foster a resilient team, and drive your dental practice towards success. We've got our work cut out for us, so let's begin.

CHAPTER 2:

Leadership

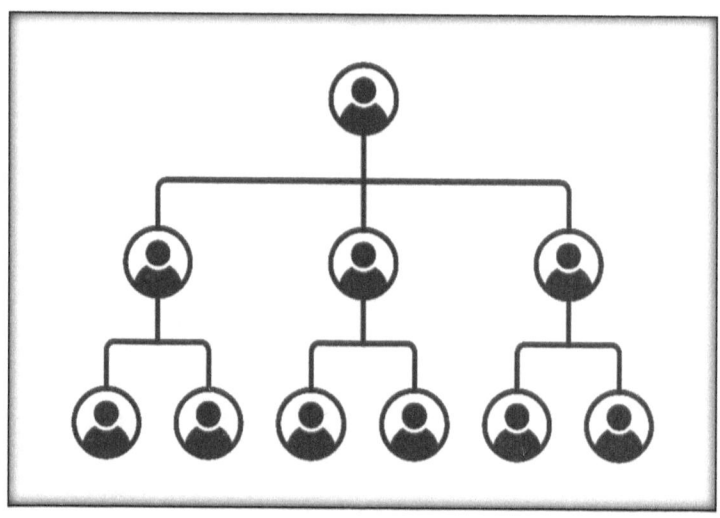

"Leadership is not about being in charge. It's about taking care of those in your charge." -
Simon Sinek

Learning Objectives

A-The need for leadership: Why becoming a leader is key to your success
B-There is more than one leadership style
C-Discovering your leadership style
D-Adapting your unique leadership style
E-Continuous evaluation of your leadership
F-Putting words into action
G-Put your team first
H-know your team members

A. The Need for Leadership: Why Becoming a Leader is Key to your Success

Leadership matters today more than ever. In a rapidly evolving world, the ability to guide and inspire others is not just a desirable trait; it is a necessity. The success of any venture hinges on effective leadership. Leaders are those who navigate through the stormy seas of obstacles and challenges, steering their teams towards success. They are the torchbearers who illuminate the path during times of uncertainty, ensuring that the journey of learning and growth never ceases.

Without strong leadership, a business may falter, lose direction, and ultimately fail to reach its potential. In the context of a dental office, the absence of effective leadership can have dire consequences.

Without clear direction, the staff may struggle to perform their duties accurately and efficiently, potentially leading to chaotic situations and mishandled patient care. Employees may exhibit a variety of adverse behaviors and attitudes. Uncertainty and confusion become prevalent, as there is no clear vision or direction guiding their actions. This can result in inefficiency and disorganization, as tasks might be duplicated or overlooked.

Morale may decrease, with employees feeling unmotivated and un-valued, as their roles and contributions lack clarity and recognition. We may also experience conflict, as there are no established protocols for decision-making or conflict resolution. Office issues can also compromise the quality of patient care, as disengaged and discontented staff are unlikely to deliver their best performance.

In a dysfunctional dental office where leadership is lacking, stress levels can skyrocket, affecting everyone involved, including the dentist. The constant uncertainty and chaos can create a high-stress environment. Staff members may feel anxious and overwhelmed due to unclear roles, unmet expectations, and lack of organizational direction. This can lead to a decrease in job satisfaction and an increase in turnover rates.

For the dentist, this translates to additional pressures. They may find themselves playing multiple roles beyond their professional capacity in an attempt to keep the office afloat. This can lead to burnout, an increased risk of making clinical errors, and a decline in the quality of patient care being provided.

An environment of unease and tension can also permeate the office, where it is felt by patients and negatively impacts their overall experience. In such an environment, instead of focusing on growth and providing excellent patient care, the energy is directed towards managing conflicts and treading water, which is both exhausting and unsustainable in the long run.

Unfortunately, I have witnessed numerous dental offices operating in a state of chaos. In these offices, written procedures are absent, communication is poor, and there is a distinct lack of direction. This pandemonium not only disrupts the work environment, but it also leads to a significant loss in production dollars.

All these challenges are due to the fact that the dentist has not stepped up to the leadership position by taking charge of the situation. I have witnessed doctors hiding from drama with their staff, letting their wives run the office, or shying away from any office challenges. When I did my predental externship with a dentist, the wife (his former RDA) was running the show and telling me how the staff don't take initiative. It's like the doctors want to run the office but without being involved. In dental school this was the only way: do your part to pass classes and clinicals and no need to run a business. But we are not in dental school anymore.

The transformation from a chaotic dental office to a well-functioning one starts with effective leadership. Leaders create a vision and inspire others to believe and achieve it. In a dental office, the dentist often assumes the leadership role, setting the tone for the team. By gaining leadership skills, dentists can better manage their team, creating a more positive and productive working environment.

Consider the case of Microsoft, which experienced a significant transformation under the leadership of Satya Nadella. When Nadella assumed the role of CEO in 2014, Microsoft was known primarily as a company focused on licensed software. However, Nadella ushered in a new era of growth and innovation. He shifted the company's focus towards cloud computing, artificial intelligence, and a more customer-centric approach. This significant change in direction was accompanied by a change in company culture. Nadella fostered an environment that encouraged learning and innovation, emphasizing the value of a growth mindset. As a result of this leadership change, Microsoft has not only become one of the leaders in the tech industry but also reinvigorated its image as an innovative and forward-thinking company. Leaders drive the direction of their companies.

B. THERE IS MORE THAN ONE LEADERSHIP STYLES

1. In the autocratic approach, leaders make decisions without consulting their team, relying solely on their own judgment and authority. This style can be effective in situations that require quick decisions and clear direction.

It may not foster a sense of teamwork or involvement, as team members may feel excluded from the decision-making process. It is important for leaders to consider the impact of their leadership style on team dynamics and adapt their approach accordingly to create a collaborative and inclusive work environment.

2. A democratic leader is known for their inclusive and collaborative approach, actively involving their team in decision-making processes. By valuing and considering the input of team members, this leadership style fosters a more harmonious work environment and promotes creativity and innovation.

This participatory approach to decision-making may sometimes result in a slightly slower pace due to the involvement of multiple perspectives and ideas. Nonetheless, the benefits of inclusivity and collaboration make this leadership style a valuable asset in modern organizations.

3. A <u>transformational leader</u>, with their inspiring and visionary approach, has the ability to ignite passion and motivation in their team members. By painting a compelling picture of the future, they empower and encourage their team to not only meet their individual performance goals but also to actively contribute to the overall success of the dental practice.

This leadership style, while impactful, demands a consistent display of charisma, and maintaining such influence over the long term can present challenges. It requires a delicate balance of leadership qualities, effective communication, and a deep understanding of the team dynamics to sustain a transformative leadership approach.

4. A <u>laissez-faire</u> leader, also known as a hands-off leader, empowers their team by providing them with the freedom to make decisions and take ownership of their work. This leadership style often fosters high levels of employee satisfaction and creativity, as team members feel trusted and valued.

This approach can sometimes lead to a lack of direction and control, which may require additional guidance and support from the leader to ensure the team stays focused and aligned with organizational goals.

It's essential to understand these styles and adapt your approach based on your personal strengths. Effective leadership is not about forcing one style onto all situations, but rather about being flexible and adaptable to ensure the success of your dental office.

C. Discovering Your Leadership Style

One of the key steps in becoming an effective leader is understanding yourself, including your strengths, weaknesses, and individual leadership style. This exploration process can be facilitated by self-reflection, seeking feedback from colleagues and team members, and even through personality and leadership assessments. Recognizing what motivates you, what types of environments you thrive in, and how you handle stress can provide a clearer picture of your leadership.

It is much easier to nurture your existing leadership style than to completely go against the grain and do a 360. Stick to your foundations and learn from it, build upon it, and make a become a better leader. There are no right, or wrong styles and all leadership are there for one purpose: to make help their followers succeed.

1. SELF-ASSESSMENT

To begin, it is crucial to gain a comprehensive understanding of your current leadership style. Take the time to assess and evaluate your strengths and weaknesses, and examine how they influence your team dynamics and overall leadership practice. This introspective analysis will empower you to make informed decisions and drive positive change within your team.

Everyone has an inherent leadership style, shaped and molded over the course of their lives and influenced by experiences from childhood through adulthood. This style often emerges naturally in various situations, from familial interactions to academic and professional settings.

If we have a negative leadership style, then we can change it to a better one. The prospect of changing your leadership style might seem daunting, but it's essential to understand that some styles may work better in certain situations than others. Each team, each employee, and each situation are unique and may necessitate a different approach. This doesn't mean you're discarding your inherent leadership style. Instead, you're becoming more well-rounded, more versatile, and more effective as a leader.

If your current style isn't yielding the results you desire, don't hesitate to adapt. Whether it involves adopting a more democratic approach to decision-making, exhibiting a more transformational style to inspire and motivate, or integrating a more coaching-oriented style to develop your team's skills. It's not about changing who you are; it's about maximizing your effectiveness in leading your team to success.

2. Feedback from Others

To gain valuable insights into your leadership style, proactively seek feedback from your team. Cultivate an open and welcoming environment that encourages them to share their candid thoughts and perceptions. Consider soliciting feedback from friends and family members. By gathering this data, you will establish a baseline for your current leadership style.

Each situation has three perspectives: how we see it ourselves, how others see it, and the actual truth. Relying solely on our own judgment or the opinions of our employees is insufficient. By seeking feedback from a diverse range of individuals, we can gain a clearer understanding of our authentic selves.

3. Identifying Areas for Improvement: The Why Must Be Answered

Based on the feedback received, take the time to carefully identify areas that require improvement. These areas may encompass enhancing communication channels to ensure seamless information flow, delegating tasks effectively to optimize productivity, and fostering an inclusive environment that welcomes and values diverse perspectives.

Pursuing self-improvement can feel futile without a compelling reason, the "why". Take a glance at gyms every January; they're bustling with individuals eager to transform their physical shape. But observe what happens by March: gym attendance returns to normal. Why does this occur? I can relate because I used to be that way. New Year's resolutions would fade after a mere two months. So, what is my true motivation for consistently going to the gym?

A couple of years ago, I experienced physical issues with my lower back and neck. Throughout the day, I struggled to turn my neck and suffered from recurring lower back pain, rendering me unable to walk for several days when I pulled a lower back muscle. Seeking medical advice, my MD suggested medication, a common response in America. However, I dismissed this approach.

It was disheartening to face such significant problems before even reaching the age of 50. I realized that if these issues persisted for another two years, my dentistry career would be in jeopardy.

Reflecting on the past, I realized that I had not encountered these problems until recently, leading me to a revelation: my muscles were weakening, and I needed to strengthen them.

Despite my dislike for the gym, I forced myself to go. Participating in challenging classes pushed me to my limits. After six months, I began noticing improvements. My body gained more mobility, and after a year, my neck had fully regained its range of motion. I understood the reason behind my efforts: if I neglected the gym, I would become unable to work.

At this point in my life, I have made a conscious decision to prioritize my health above all else. Recognizing the significance it holds, I have committed myself to dedicating 3-4 days every week to go to the gym, ensuring that I invest ample time and effort in maintaining my physical well-being. As a result, I understand that some of my other activities may need to take a backseat, as I prioritize my fitness journey and strive to maintain a healthy lifestyle.

Without the "why" we fail. In January of every year, the gyms are packed with people. Their new year's resolution is to lose what and become more in shape, of course more attractive. But is that the "why?" The reasoning is not strong enough and 90% of the New Year New Me people will stop going to the gym in on or before March. Unless someone has a strong enough reason like not being able to work anymore, going to the gym becomes another chore.

4. EDUCATION AND TRAINING

To further enhance your leadership skills, I highly recommend actively seeking out valuable resources, such as books, seminars, and online courses. Engaging in continuous learning is an essential aspect of leadership development, as it allows you to stay up-to-date with the latest trends and practices in the field.

Life's experiences can significantly aid in leadership. Having traveled to 30 countries, some of which I had the privilege of living in, I have gained valuable insights into diverse ways of life and conducting business. For instance, my upbringing in small-town America, specifically Yuba City, led me to believe that we had a good public transportation system. However, when I visited Europe, I was astounded by the efficiency and sustainability of their public transportation. The electric trains, in particular, were phenomenal.

Experiencing new things in life can indeed broaden our perspectives and enhance our leadership methodologies. Each new environment we encounter, every unique culture we immerse ourselves in, and every novel challenge we face allows us to grow and expand our philosophy of leadership. We begin to understand that there isn't one 'right' way of doing things but a plethora of approaches, each best tailored to specific situations and teams. For example, a leadership technique that may work exceptionally well in a high-pressure corporate environment may not be as effective in a small, close-knit dental office.

By dedicating time and effort to expand your knowledge and expertise, you can effectively grow as a leader and make a lasting impact in your professional journey.

5. SEEKING MENTORSHIP AND COACHING

An effective method to accelerate your leadership growth journey is to seek the guidance of a mentor or coach. This could be a seasoned leader in your field or a professional coach who specializes in leadership development. They can provide you with personalized advice, constructive feedback, and strategies tailored to your unique needs and goals. They can help you gain a fresh perspective on your challenges and guide you in navigating them effectively. Even the best leaders never stop learning, and having a mentor or coach can be a valuable asset in your continuous pursuit of leadership excellence.

One of the most influential mentors in Warren Buffett's life was Benjamin Graham, often hailed as the "father of value investing." Graham was not only Buffett's professor at Columbia Business School but also his boss at Graham-Newman Corporation. His teachings on investing strategy and philosophy greatly shaped Buffett's approach to business and leadership. Buffett has often credited Graham's guidance as an integral part of his success, highlighting the importance of mentorship in the journey of leadership.

In the realm of basketball, Michael Jordan's name is synonymous with excellence and success. Phil Jackson coached the Chicago Bulls from 1989 to 1998 and was pivotal in leading the team to six championships during this period. His unique coaching style, centered around fostering a team-oriented, selfless approach to the game, had a profound influence on Jordan. The mutual trust and respect between Jordan and Jackson played a crucial role in the Bulls' dominance in the 90s.

D. Adapting Your Unique Leadership Style

After gaining valuable insight into your leadership style and carefully identifying specific areas for improvement, you can begin to adapt your style accordingly. For instance, during times of crisis, you might find it necessary to adopt a more *autocratic approach*, providing clear direction and making decisive decisions to navigate through challenges. On the other hand, when your team requires creative freedom to flourish, a more *laissez-faire approach* could be beneficial, fostering an environment that encourages innovation and independent thinking.

Leadership often demands a delicate balance between remaining calm and taking decisive action. As a leader, it is essential to maintain a composed demeanor even in the face of adversity. This not only instills confidence in your team but also aids in clear-headed decision-making.

However, being calm should never be mistaken for a lack of courage or decisiveness. There will be situations where you need to step up, make tough calls, and take charge. A successful leader is not one who shies away from challenges or disagreements.

Instead, they embrace these as opportunities for learning and growth. They command respect by their decisiveness and earn loyalty through their steadfastness. So, while tranquility is valuable in leadership, becoming a 'gutless' leader is not an option if you wish to see your dental practice thrive.

E. CONTINUOUS EVALUATION OF YOUR LEADERSHIP

Leadership development is a continuous and ever-evolving journey. It involves regularly assessing your progress, seeking valuable feedback from others, and making necessary adjustments to ensure that you are effectively leading and steering your dental practice towards long-term success.

By actively investing in your growth, you can cultivate the necessary skills, knowledge, and mindset to inspire and empower your team, foster a positive work culture, and deliver exceptional patient care.

One of the hardest things to accept as a leader, yet undeniably crucial, is that making mistakes is a part of the journey. No leader is infallible, and in the intricate world of a dental office, errors are bound to happen. Instead of regarding these as failures, consider them as steppingstones towards improvement.

They provide valuable lessons that can help you refine your strategies, improve decision-making, and enhance your leadership qualities. The mistake itself is not what defines you as a leader. It's how you react, learn, and grow from it that truly matters. When you stumble—and you will—pick yourself up, learn the lesson, and stride forward with renewed confidence and determination.

F. Putting Words into Action

Leaders should also be mindful of the importance of modeling the behaviors they expect from their team. For example, punctuality is a key aspect of professionalism in any workplace. If a leader is strict about punctuality but regularly comes in late, it sends a mixed message to the team. This "do as I say, not as I do" approach can lead to confusion, resentment, and a lack of respect for leadership. Maintaining consistency between your actions and expectations is crucial to build trust and establish a positive and productive work environment in your dental practice.

Consider another scenario in which a team member in your dental practice, who has been with you for several years, is asking for a well-deserved raise. Despite their hard work and dedication, you deny their request, citing financial constraints. Interestingly, you are driving a new luxury car every two years, which raises questions about the fairness and transparency.

The discrepancy between what you say and what you do raises significant questions about your integrity as a leader. When your words and actions are not aligned, it can create a sense of unfairness and de-motivation among your team members. They may question your authenticity.

By aligning your words and actions, you establish a strong foundation of trust and reliability. Remember, as a leader, your actions often speak louder than your words. It is through your actions that you can truly inspire and motivate your team to achieve greatness.

The most exceptional leaders are those who possess the remarkable ability to adapt their leadership style to perfectly align with the unique needs of their team and the ever-evolving demands of their practice.

By carefully observing and understanding their team members' strengths, weaknesses, and motivations, these adaptable leaders can tailor their approach to bring out the best in each individual. This nuanced understanding allows them to foster an environment of trust, collaboration, and growth, ultimately driving unparalleled success for their team and organization as a whole.

G. Put Your Team First

As leaders, particularly in a dental practice, prioritizing people over profits is a fundamental principle for sustainable success. This isn't merely a feel-good mantra; it is a strategic approach that focuses on the wellbeing of your employees and patients. When your team feels valued and respected, they are more likely to deliver exceptional service, fostering patient satisfaction and loyalty.

If your sole focus in life was to accumulate wealth and financial success, you might have considered pursuing a career in the stock market or becoming a hedge fund manager. In this line of work, your primary responsibility would be maximizing profits without necessarily having to prioritize the wellbeing of others. As long as the returns were substantial, your clients would have been immensely satisfied with the results you delivered. This path could have provided you with ample opportunities to thrive in the world of finance and establish a reputation as a skilled wealth creator.

Instead, you chose dentistry. This choice speaks volumes about your commitment to serving people and making a tangible difference in their lives. As a dentist and a leader, you are not just treating teeth, you are offering comfort, restoring confidence, and promoting overall health. Your role goes beyond financial transactions to form meaningful relationships with patients and employees based on trust, empathy, and understanding. In this profession, success is not just measured by the bottom line, but by the smiles you brighten, the lives you improve, and the team you inspire.

Profits naturally arise from a well-managed practice. A leader who genuinely cares for their team and patients not only cultivates a thriving dental practice but also generates a favorable cash flow for the office.

Even though we give the patients the benefits of the doubt, your team comes first with some patients. These patients may be rude, have mental challenges, or just want to take the office time without actually getting any treatment completed. Let me explain about this with one such patient.

Elderly patient comes to the office, walks in for an appointment. This is rare because most patients call to make the first appointment. He seems ok at first. Then once he is on the schedule, he sends my office information about UFO's and other conspiracy theories. The main reason that he came in was of a broke tooth number 4. After the exam, Diagnoses was fractured tooth at the gum line with a root tip infection. Treatment was extraction and implant. I thought that was the end of that.

He did not want to take care of his broken tooth but wanted a complete exam of the rest of his mouth. So 3 days later we see him on the schedule. After my assistant takes the complete X-rays, it was my time to go in.

I completed my exam and his mouth did not look at bad, a couple of crowns with some fillings and deep cleaning. It was understanding since he had not gone to a dentist for almost 10 years. But during the exam, he wanted to tell me about the surgery and the issues that he was having with his right shoulder.

He was talking and after 5 minutes, it was not getting anywhere. I felt like he needed a person to talk to so I stopped him a couple of times and he asked me that there is a point to this. Fast forward, he was under the care of physicians for his right shoulder and he asked me if the antibiotics that the had put him on had any negative side affects.

All antibiotics have a good and bad side but I did not want to get into the antibiotic issue with him because that was out the scope of my field. He is here in my office for his mouth, I cannot do anything about his shoulder. So the next treatment was his initial treatment of removing the bad tooth and placing an implant. Did he schedule?

No way. He told the staff that he is changing insurances and that he needs to wait. That's fine. But now he is sending our office with useless information about everything under the sun. How I knew this: the staff complains about his communication all the time.

Judging from experience, this patient does not want to spend the money to get the dental implant nor anything else. He wants to find an office who will sympathize with his needs and his shoulder. We need to keep these patients at bay or else they will consume the time of our office without getting any treatment done.

The other challenge arises when team members become sick. This was not a big issue before Covid but it seems that people are getting sick more. I have experienced more sick days and some of my hardest working team members. So what do we do when the team becomes sick.

First take a deep breath, we can do this. A couple of days of slow production will not hurt anything. Two, assess the situation to see if we need to reschedule some patients. If you have a 5-member team, your office is super busy, and 2 team members call in sick, then the schedule must be reduced a little bit. We reschedule all the small non urgent appointments like crown seats and fillings. We keep the large appointments because there is less running around, setting up the room, and so forth.

The truth of the matter is that if a team member is sick, it's better that they stay from others. If they come in then they get the entire office sick now instead of losing 5 days from one team member, you might be looking at losing 5 days from all the team. Then the team's family will get sick and team members may have to stay home to take care of their children. Whenever our team members become sick, we tell them to stay home.

It's harder to find great team members than to find patients. Patients are a dime a dozen, they really need you when they have or you take their insurances. Some are cool but patients are not our best friends but they are a paying customer. We provide them service and they reimburse us. But without great employees our practice would go nowhere.

H. KNOW YOUR TEAM MEMBERS

Effective leadership in a dental practice extends beyond clinical competency and business acumen. It requires an in-depth understanding of your team members, including their strengths, weaknesses, aspirations, and fears. Taking the time to know your staff at a personal level fosters a sense of belonging and encourages open communication. Make it a point to engage in regular one-on-one meetings or performance reviews, providing constructive feedback and taking note of their career goals or personal interests.

Equipped with this knowledge, you can delegate tasks more effectively, playing to each member's strengths, and provide support where necessary. This personalized approach not only builds trust and respect but also boosts morale and productivity, contributing to the overall success of your dental practice. Remember, to lead is to serve, and understanding your team is a crucial element of servant leadership.

The other day, our schedule was unexpectedly slow, and we found ourselves with a leisurely 2-hour lunch block. Seizing the opportunity, I decided to treat my team members to lunch. Normally, there are more of us, but on this particular day, our numbers were slightly diminished due to one member being out sick, another being on maternity leave, and a third enjoying a well-deserved vacation.

There were two new employees who recently joined our team, and I didn't know much about them, especially the quite girl working in the front office. So that a perfect opportunity to take them to lunch and learn about them.

What I learned during our lunch was that one of them was having family issues and needed to help her family during these difficult times, while the other was embarking on a new chapter in her life by moving out for the first time. The first one loves K-pop, and the second loves cats.

In the week that followed, I started to notice a palpable shift in the office atmosphere. Both of the new team members seemed far more engaged and willing to help out. This boosted morale and fostered a stronger sense of camaraderie within our team.

Clearly, investing that time into understanding them on a personal level not only enriched our work relationships but also positively impacted the overall productivity and atmosphere of our dental practice. This only reinforces the truth: effective leadership is anchored in empathy and understanding.

During our regular group meetings, both young women shared their positive experiences of working with us. They expressed how much they love being part of our team, appreciating the calm and organized environment we've cultivated here. They credited this serene atmosphere to the efficient leadership and thoughtfully implemented systems that keep our operations running smoothly.

The importance of spending quality time with my team cannot be over stressed. This experience offered more than just an opportunity to enjoy a meal together; it was about understanding their individual situations, challenges, and aspirations. Connecting with them on a personal level allowed me to comprehend their motivations better and to appreciate the unique perspectives they bring to our dental office.

This enriched understanding is instrumental in fostering a supportive and empathetic working environment where everyone feels valued and heard. It's this environment that drives our collective success and underpins the strength of our leadership within the dental industry.

Summary

Effective leadership in a dental practice, or any organization, is about more than just managing tasks and procedures. It is about connecting with your team on a personal level, understanding their individual challenges and motivations, and fostering an environment of empathy and support. This not only boosts morale and productivity but also nurtures a culture where everyone feels valued and heard. It is this approach that drives collective success and distinguishes exceptional leaders in the dental industry and beyond.

CHAPTER 3:

Office Vision

"The only thing worse than being blind is having sight but no vision." -
Helen Keller

LEARNING OBJECTIVES

A-Planning equals vision
B-Your vision: A guiding light for others
C-Creating a vision and a vision statement
D-Key components of the office vision
E-Some Examples of Vision Statement
F-Implementing the vision
G-Money and it's affects in the office
H-Work family
I-Nothing stays the same

A well-defined vision is the foundational pillar that informs all future decisions and practices within the office. Therefore, the first step towards successful leadership in a dental practice, or any business, is developing a clear and compelling vision. Vision is the guiding light that gives direction to the entire team, outlining the goals, values, and ambition of the organization. It provides a path to follow, as well as the motivation to embark on that journey.

In the initial years of your dental practice, your focus might be predominantly on mastering your craft, expanding your clientele, and establishing a strong reputation in the industry. As you mature both personally and professionally, your vision might evolve to prioritizing team development, fostering a positive work culture, focusing on patient satisfaction, and achieving a balance between work and personal life.

In the later stages, you might shift towards mentoring the next generation of dentists, giving back to your community, or even exploring new business ventures. No matter the stage, it's crucial to align your vision with your core values and to be ready to adapt as you continue to grow.

A leader's vision for a dental practice might encompass the standard of care they wish to offer, the working environment they aim to create, the reputation they desire in the community, and how they intend to achieve growth. Crafting this vision requires introspection, an understanding of the healthcare industry, and a strong desire to make a positive impact.

A vision statement, in essence, provides a clear roadmap for your team and sets the direction for your business's growth. In this chapter, I will discuss how to develop one for your office.

I will use vision and vision statement interchangeably here, as the only difference is that your vision is what you have inside your head, while your vision statement is what is written for others to see and follow.

A. Planning Equals Vision

Having a clear vision for your office is akin to taking a well-planned vacation. When embarking on a trip, you don't simply pack your bags and leave without direction. Arriving at your destination, you don't want to be caught up in the frenzy of searching for a suitable hotel or deciding which sights to explore. Such a haphazard approach not only wastes precious time but also increases stress and detracts from the overall enjoyment of your vacation. Most dentists don't have a vision for their offices. They come to work, do their dentistry, and leave for the day.

After finishing our first year of dental school, my buddy and I decided to do a backpacking trip in Europe. The only thing we got were the plane tickets, and we planned to figure everything else out once we got there. Needless to say, we encountered some challenges. Once, we wanted to get to a specific country location, but all the train seats were sold out, so we had to come back another day. In Pamplona, Spain, where the running of the bulls and the tomato festival takes place, we arrived to discover that there were no hotel rooms. So, we ended up renting a room in an old home. Looking back, we wasted a lot of time, but we were young and had 6 weeks to kill. Today when I travel, it's usually a week or less, so I cannot waste any time.

Planning your vacation ahead of time can save you countless hours of searching once you arrive, allowing you to fully enjoy your time there. From transportation and flights to hotels, dining options, sightseeing, and tours, along with scheduled rest days, your trip becomes not only fun but also truly relaxing. With a solid game plan in place, you can optimize your travel experience and make the most of every moment. Like a well-planned vacation, a well-crafted vision will ultimately lead to a successful and fulfilling journey in which your dental practice thrives and prospers.

B. Your Vision: A Guiding Light for Others

Leadership goes beyond just managing tasks; it is about directing others towards the realization of a common vision. A leader is like a compass, providing direction and guidance to the team. This involves not only setting clear, achievable goals but also providing the necessary resources and support to achieve those goals.

A leader needs to effectively communicate the vision, inspire their team to believe in it, and motivate them to work towards it. They need to create an atmosphere in which every team member feels they are contributing to the achievement of the shared vision. When a leader successfully directs others in this manner, it fosters team cohesion and enhances the overall productivity of the dental office.

A leader's vision is paramount to the success of a dental office. It serves as a guiding light, illuminating the path that the team should follow. The vision should be clear, compelling, and accurately reflect the core values and objectives of the practice. If you are not sure about the path of your office, your team won't be either.

Moreover, a vision is futile if it's not effectively communicated to your team. A true leader skillfully articulates their vision, ensuring it resonates with everyone in a way that they can understand and embrace. This is no small task. It requires clarity in communication, empathy to understand different perspectives, and patience to address queries and doubts.

Once the vision is communicated, it's the leader's responsibility to ensure that it's translated into achievable goals. They must provide the necessary resources and support to enable their team to work towards these goals. They need to foster a sense of shared purpose, where every team member feels valued and understands that their contributions are pivotal in realizing the shared vision. This shared vision fuels the team's motivation, boosts morale, and drives the dental practice towards success.

C. Creating a Vision and a Vision Statement

To begin, think about the kinds of dental services you want to provide and which ones you want to refer out. Do you aspire to be the best family-friendly dental office in your town? Or, perhaps, you want to specialize in cosmetic dentistry? Once you've identified this, consider the values that underpin your practice. These values could include patient satisfaction, quality service, continuous learning, or community involvement.

Next, consider your long-term goals. Where do you see your dental office in 5, 10, or even 20 years? Are there any specific milestones you want to hit? This could be expanding your office, employing a set number of staff, reaching a certain level of profitability, or receiving a prestigious industry award.

Once you have a handle on these aspects, you can craft your vision statement. A *vision statement* is a succinct, inspiring phrase that encapsulates your practice's purpose and future aspirations. It should be motivational for your staff and reassuring for your patients.

Your vision should be flexible enough to adapt to changes in the industry or your local area. It's not set in stone, and as a leader, you should be open to adjusting it as necessary. The most important thing is that it always reflects your core values and long-term objectives, guiding all your decisions and actions in your dental practice.

D. Key Components of an Office Vision

1. **Understanding Your Mission:** This is the fundamental reason why your dental office exists. It's the core purpose that drives every activity and decision, ensuring the oral health and wellbeing of your patients. With a commitment to providing high-quality dental care, your office strives to create healthy and beautiful smiles, while promoting overall dental hygiene and preventive measures.

2. **Identifying Your Values:** These guiding principles are the core beliefs that form the foundation of your practice, setting you apart from other dental offices. They shape your approach to patient care, emphasizing a personalized and compassionate experience. What 3-5 areas are you passionate about? Clean office, well-treat staff, being content, etc.?

3. **Defining Your Goals:** These measurable and achievable targets are specific objectives that you set for yourself, aiming to reach them within a specified time frame. With your goals

defined, you can effectively track your progress and stay motivated on your path to success.

4. Crafting Your Vision Statement: This succinct and inspiring phrase encapsulates the core purpose and future aspirations of your dental practice. It serves as a motivational reminder for your dedicated staff while providing reassurance and comfort to your valued patients.

5. Implementing Your Vision: This involves carefully crafting and implementing comprehensive strategies and plans that align perfectly with your long-term vision, ensuring that they are specifically tailored to help you successfully achieve your goals and aspirations.

6. Aligning Your Team: It is crucial to ensure that your team fully understands and aligns with your vision. They should not only be motivated by it but also feel inspired to work collaboratively towards making it a reality. You can encourage your team members to bring their unique skills and perspectives to the table, contributing to the collective success and growth of the organization. Together, you can create a thriving environment where everyone feels valued and empowered to make a meaningful impact.

7. Evaluating and Adjusting Your Vision: As time goes by and the industry or local area evolves, it is crucial to regularly reassess and fine-tune your vision to ensure that it remains aligned with your core values and long-term objectives, adapting to the changing landscape while staying true to your principles.

E. Some Examples of Vision Statements

1. **"Enhancing Dental Health, One Smile at a Time"** This vision statement clearly conveys a commitment to improving the overall dental health of patients. It implies an emphasis on thorough and personalized dental care, cultivating an image of a dental practice that takes the time to address individual patient needs.

2. **"Leading Innovation in Oral Healthcare"** A vision of this nature suggests a practice that is at the forefront of the latest advancements in dental technology and treatments. It evokes a sense of progress and adaptability, indicating a practice that is dedicated to providing the most cutting-edge care.

3. **"Creating a Generation of Confident Smiles"** A vision statement like this speaks to a practice that not only focuses on oral health but also on the self-esteem of patients. It indicates an awareness of the significant role oral health plays in a person's overall confidence and wellbeing.

F. Implementing the Vision

After we have our vision and vision statement, it's time to communicate this information to our team.

1. **Articulate Your Vision:** When communicating your vision to the team, it is crucial to do so with clarity and passion. By using simple and straightforward language, you can ensure that your message is easily understood and not misinterpreted. This will help create a shared understanding and alignment among team members, fostering a collaborative and productive

environment. Each individual may bring a unique perspective to the table, so take the time to tailor your message in a way that resonates with everyone, regardless of their specific role within the dental practice.

2. Hold a Team Meeting: It is essential to call a team meeting. This gathering not only emphasizes the importance of your message but also provides an opportunity for everyone to hear it simultaneously. By bringing the entire team together, you create a collaborative atmosphere where ideas can be shared and discussed, fostering a sense of unity and alignment towards a common goal. It also allows for real-time feedback and clarification, ensuring that everyone is on the same page and fully understands the vision you are conveying.

Utilize visual cues such as a well-crafted PowerPoint presentation or a written document to ensure that they can easily comprehend and retain the information.

3. Encourage Feedback: After presenting your vision, it is crucial to create an environment that encourages open dialogue, allowing for any potential misunderstandings to be clarified in a collaborative manner. This provides an opportunity for team members to contribute their perspectives and insights, which may lead to the discovery of better ideas or previously overlooked aspects.

4. Translate the Vision into Goals: To effectively execute your vision, it is crucial to break it down into achievable goals. Provide your team with a clear roadmap, enabling them to understand their individual contributions towards realizing the vision. Consider assigning specific due dates for each step or part of the process to ensure timely progress and accountability. This comprehensive approach fosters clarity, motivation, and a shared sense of purpose among team members, ultimately leading to the successful realization of your vision.

5. Regularly Reinforce the Vision: Continually reminding your team about the vision and the progress towards it is crucial for maintaining motivation and keeping the vision at the forefront of their activities. This is especially important in the first 30 days, as it sets the foundation for success and establishes a strong sense of direction.

G. Money and It's Affects in the Office

Money: The root of all evil or a means to get things. Money has often been labeled as the root of all evil, a viewpoint that tends to associate wealth with greed, corruption, and other negative implications. However, money is just a tool to exchange value in our society, as the days of bartering are long gone.

While monetary compensation is important for the team, it is not their primary motivation. Team members are driven by a variety of factors, such as a sense of accomplishment, the desire to make a difference, the opportunity for growth and development, and a supportive and engaging work environment. The are looking for a work family.

It is important to recognize that the owner is typically the hardest working individual in the business. With the most at stake, their level of dedication often exceeds that of any team member. While monetary gain may be the primary motivator for most owners, the same cannot be said for the team members.

H. WORK FAMILY

Many dental team members spend more time with their office family than they do with their own families. As a result, the bonds formed in a dental office often mirror familial relationships. The environment becomes a blend of professional and personal, fostering camaraderie, mutual respect, and the willingness to go above and beyond. This "work family" concept can be a powerful tool in building a successful and thriving dental practice. The key is to nurture this dynamic and allow it to flourish organically. This is more achievable in small one-doctor dental offices than in large corporate ones.

A dental office, like any other workplace, thrives on a sense of community and belonging. If the only incentive you provide your team is monetary, you may not be able to retain them for long. Money is certainly crucial, but it's far from the only thing that matters to your staff. Most people want to feel like they are part of a "work family," where they are respected, valued, and heard. They yearn for meaningful relationships, a strong work culture, and a sense of purpose in what they do. If your team feels like they are merely cogs in a machine, without any emotional connection or personal growth, they are more likely to leave, even earning less money at another office.

On the flip side, if the work is toxic, it can shatter team morale and productivity. Imagine walking into the office every day only to be met with negativity, petty disputes, and constant tension. This kind of atmosphere can make even the most dedicated team members consider leaving. The impact of such toxicity seeps into their personal life, making it difficult for them to stay motivated or perform their best. A negative work environment can spell disaster for a dental office, regardless of how skilled or experienced the practitioners might be.

I. NOTHING STAYS THE SAME

Embracing the concept that "nothing is set in stone" is intrinsic to dynamic leadership in a dental office setting. It is pivotal to remember that the strategies, goals, and even the vision you set for your practice can change as the circumstances do.

For example, let's say that you had a great family life and now a divorce occurs. You may have to sell your office or buy your spouse out. Or maybe a key team member in your office are no longer present. The initial vision that you had are not viable anymore; thus, it's time for new ones. Be ready to learn and unlearn, and modify your plans based on new circumstances.

Over the years, my vision for my office has undergone a remarkable transformation. Initially, my sole emphasis was on ambitious growth, continuous development, and a tireless work ethic that had me dedicating six days a week to diligently tackling my financial debts head-on. With each passing day, I strived to create a prosperous workspace. Through persistence and unwavering determination, I gradually shaped my office into my dreams.

But the price of success took a toll on my health: working long hours, not exercising much, and many visits to happy hours at restaurants and bars had beaten me down. I was tired of that lifestyle and needed a change, and I think my team was on the same page.

Today is a stark departure from the yesteryears. My focus now lies in prioritizing the wellbeing of both myself and my team. Instead of rushing from room to room, I dedicate ample time to being present with patients and my team. This deliberate approach allows me to forge stronger connections and deliver exceptional dental care.

I carefully select which cases and patients to take and which ones to refer out. While I used to attempt to treat kids, our office just isn't equipped for it. I often couldn't complete the procedures because the kids would cry excessively, leading us to stop and refer them elsewhere. It was a significant waste of office time. Now, I refer them out right from the start, recognizing and respecting my limitations.

Every morning, I gather my team for a quick huddle. We discuss the day's agenda and align our efforts. It's incredible how smooth our days turn out now, a vast improvement from the previous chaotic times. Of course, considering the nature of our business, the remaining 10% of abnormality is probably impossible to avoid. Personally, I find these ratios perfectly acceptable.

Summary

In this section we have discussed planning and the vision. How to create one and communicated this with your team to hit your target. We have talked about the parts of a vision statement and gave some examples.

Money is the everyone's driving force and we need to find what drives each of your team members. Working with your team for a long time gives a sense of family and we must not forget that nothing stays the same.

As we navigate the various stages of our business life, our vision and leadership style can indeed undergo significant shifts. We cannot achieve any lasting success without being a great communicator and that is covered in the next chapter.

CHAPTER 4:

Becoming a Great Communicator

"Communication—the human connection—is the key to personal and career success." - *Paul J. Meyer.*

Learning Objectives

A-Why being a great communicator is key to leadership
B-How to become an effective communicator
C-Steps in actively listening to people
D-Body language
E-Feedback
F-Consistency

As dentists, we often find ourselves in a unique predicament when it comes to communication. Our primary training is focused on oral health, not interpersonal communication. We spend countless hours studying and mastering the art of dental care, perfecting our skills on teeth that, quite conveniently, don't talk back. This might lead some to believe that communication isn't as crucial in our field as it is in others. However, the reality is far from this.

A. Why Being a Great Communicator is Key to Leadership

Effective communication is a cornerstone of successful leadership, especially in a dental office setting. We must not only communicate clearly with our team but also foster an environment that encourages open dialogue. We need to listen, understand, and respond in a manner that shows empathy and respect. These communication skills are not inherent; they must be honed and developed, much like our dental expertise. Ensuring that our patients and team feel heard and understood is just as important as providing top-notch dental care. It's a challenging aspect of dentistry, but mastering it is key to leading a successful dental office.

I have noticed a profound transformation in our team dynamics since honing my communication skills. My journey towards becoming an effective communicator has inspired our team to elevate their own communication abilities. This growth has resulted in a more cohesive and collaborative environment where every team member feels valued and heard. Their increased confidence in expressing their ideas and concerns contributes to our mutual success, creating an atmosphere where everyone is equally invested in the wellbeing of our patients and the success of our dental practice.

One significant area of improvement is their ability to explain treatment plans to our patients. This used to be a task I handled exclusively, taking time away from my primary responsibilities. While I still initiate the treatment plan for a patient, my team members have become adept at addressing any additional questions the patients may have.

You know how it goes with patients. The doctor diagnoses an issue and creates a treatment plan. We then present this plan to the patient. Afterward, we ask if they have any questions, and most of them respond with a "no." However, once we leave the operatory, some patients will approach the assistant or front office with their questions. Thus, having a team who can respond to these questions with knowledge and confidence is a great asset.

B. How to Become an Effective Communicator

1. Talk in 8th Grade Level

When communicating, it is important to be clear and concise. Avoid using technical jargon; instead, opt for simple and understandable language. This will ensure that your message resonates with a wider audience and is easily comprehended by all. Don't repeat the message over and over. State it a couple of times, and allow the listener to digest it.

2. Active Listening

It's important to give your undivided attention to the speaker and demonstrate empathy. Show genuine interest in their words, actively listen, and try to understand their perspective. It takes energy to listen actively, and sometimes we don't want to do it. But we need to for a few minutes in order to proceed with effective communication.

There are countless moments in the day-to-day operations of a dental office when the value of listening becomes evident. In team meetings, casual office conversations, or one-on-one discussions, you can gain invaluable insights by simply listening to your team members.

Active listening involves not just hearing the words spoken, but also interpreting the underlying sentiments, ideas, or concerns. It takes more effort and energy to listen to someone actively, and the more we do, the less we want to. But it comes with the job and one day you will retire from the field of dentistry and never have to listen to anyone again.

If you have listened to patients for decades, you can guess their why their teeth are in that state. They may give you a long and sad story about the lack of proper oral care growing up, neglect on their part, and other reasons that has caused their teeth to become bad. Patients think that if they share their story, we dentist will treat them different, treat them better. But this is not the case because we need to see what problem they have and how can we solve it and get paid.

An experienced clinician can diagnose a simple problem and have a treatment plan within a few minutes, but patients think that telling us their long stories will change something. Maybe they want sympathy.

In any case, it is important that we make a conscious effort to listen to them. In instances that are straightforward, we can allocate a time frame of 5-10 minutes, while intricate cases will require a more substantial amount of time. Listening more than 15 minutes to a patient will kill your production time and we must learn how to keep conversations short and professional.

C. Steps in Actively Listening to People

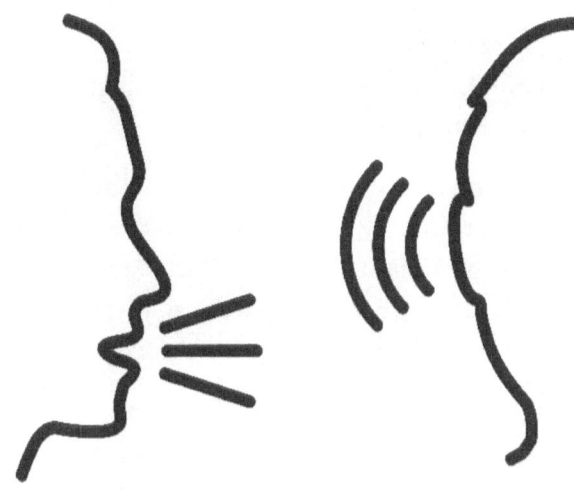

1. **Fully Engage:** Be present in the conversation. Make eye contact, and give your undivided attention to the person speaking. Avoid multitasking or letting your mind wander to other tasks.

2. **Reflect and Paraphrase:** After the speaker has shared their story or concern, paraphrase and reflect what they've said back to them. This shows that you're processing their words and helps ensure you've understood correctly.

3. **Ask Open-Ended Questions:** Encourage the speaker to elaborate more on their thoughts or feelings by asking open-ended questions. This fosters a deeper understanding and makes the speaker feel heard.

4. Avoid Interruptions: Allow the speaker to finish their thoughts before you respond. Interrupting can make them feel disrespected and could disrupt the flow of the conversation.

5. Offer Empathy and Understanding: Active listening isn't just about understanding the words; it's about understanding the emotions behind them. Validate their feelings, and show empathy in your responses.

While it's essential to listen actively, it's also crucial to manage your time effectively. Therefore, having a set time frame for listening to others can be beneficial. You could use a simple timer or note the time when the conversation starts. Once the time is up, you should aim to wrap up the conversation in a respectful and supportive manner.

Summarize the key points shared, acknowledge the speaker's feelings and thoughts, and express your gratitude for their openness. If action steps are necessary, discuss those briefly, and assure them that their concerns or suggestions will be taken into account. Remember, concluding a conversation well leaves a lasting impression and helps in fostering trust and understanding within your dental office team.

D. Body Language

Non-verbal cues, which include facial expressions, eye contact, and posture, are crucial elements that greatly influence communication. These subtle yet powerful signals can convey emotions, intentions, and attitudes, complementing the spoken words. Always position yourself in an open body posture because this gives the image of a welcoming person.

The positioning of one's body during a conversation can send various signals, impacting the overall perception of the message delivered. A few key positions to consider include:

1. Standing or Sitting Straight: Maintaining an upright position communicates confidence, attentiveness, and respect towards the speaker. An open chest and relaxed shoulders suggest that you are receptive and open to the conversation.

2. Leaning In: Leaning slightly towards the speaker shows interest and engagement in the conversation. However, be cautious not to invade the speaker's personal space, as that could come off as aggressive or uncomfortable.

3. Crossed Versus Uncrossed Arms: Crossing your arms can often signal defensiveness or closed-mindedness. In contrast, keeping your arms at your side or using them expressively can suggest openness and enthusiasm.

4. Mirroring: Subconsciously mimicking the speaker's body language can create a sense of rapport and empathy. It can show that you are on the same page and understand their perspective.

While body language is vital, its interpretation can vary based on cultural norms and individual habits. Consider the complete context before drawing conclusions. A successful dental office leader recognizes these nuances and is able to adapt their body language to foster effective and empathetic communication within the team.

E. Feedback

Encourage feedback from both your team members and patients. This creates an environment in which everyone feels comfortable expressing their thoughts and opinions, ensuring that your message is clearly understood and opening up a valuable two-way communication channel. Through this exchange of ideas, you can gather valuable insights, address any concerns, and ultimately build stronger relationships.

Create an environment where everyone feels comfortable and empowered to share their thoughts, ideas, and concerns. By showing respect for everyone's opinions, regardless of their role in the office, you can encourage open dialogue and collaboration. This not only promotes a sense of belonging and trust, but it also brings diverse perspectives to the table, leading to more innovative and effective solutions.

Listening does not necessarily imply agreement or immediate action in response to requests. Others may not have the full context or a comprehensive understanding of the situation. As the leader and owner of your dental practice, the final decision rests with you. By striking a delicate balance between being approachable and maintaining your authority, you pave the way towards the success of your dental office.

F. Consistency

Consistency is key when it comes to delivering your message. If we change the way we respond from one person to the next, then people will not know where we stand; thus, they will not trust us 100% like politicians. Also, it is difficult for them follow our lead because they cannot predict what action we may prefer. This is important when delegating tasks. If team members know you well, they can predict your response, and thus handle many tasks on your behalf. By maintaining a consistent tone, style, and focus, you establish trust and reliability, which helps to ensure that everyone involved is aligned and working towards a common goal.

SUMMARY

Effective communication is a journey, not a destination. It requires continuous learning and practice. The investment will pay dividends in terms of better leadership, a more cohesive team, and a more successful dental office.

Communication is not a dictatorship; it is a two-way street. Being a boss is not about giving directions and expecting them to be followed blindly. There are times when we need to speak less and listen more. This allows us to understand the needs, concerns, and ideas of others better. When we open our ears and mind to others, we show respect for their views and encourage a more collaborative environment. The wisdom to listen is one of the most potent features of effective leadership.

CHAPTER 5:

Creating a Team

*"Individually, we are one drop.
Together, we are an ocean." –
Ryunosuke Satoro*

Learning Objectives

A. My Learning Mistakes
B. The team will watch your back
C. Building a Great Dental Team: a Concise Guide
D. Identify and focus on each person's skills and potential
E. Guide towards self-improvement
F. Stop micromanaging

A. My Learning Mistakes

Reflecting on my personal life, I can affirm that some of my most valuable lessons have been derived from mistakes. These missteps, initially perceived as setbacks, have consistently played a role in reshaping my life for the better.

One particular incident comes to mind: I decided to open my office on Saturdays due to the high demand from patients. There were many patients who wanted to come on Saturdays because they worked during the weekdays. So we opened two Saturdays a month and the results were not good.

Turns out, few of the patients actually showed up, only 2 patients per day. Talk about a major miscalculation! Not only did this blunder fail to achieve what I had hoped for, but it also caused some tension within the office and led to some awesome team members leaving. Lesson learned: I failed to realize that team members need their own time to spend with friends and loved ones. Let's face it, no one cares about the business as much as the owner does, but the owner can't do everything alone. Now when I change anything, I ask for input before proceeding.

B. The Team Will Watch Your Back

The sheer volume of tasks, from patient care to office administration, is simply too much for one person to manage effectively. Attempting to do so can lead to burnout and detract from the quality of service offered to patients.

Leadership is about producing more leaders, not more followers. Understanding that your staff is fully capable of running 80-90% of the operations. This might include tasks like scheduling appointments, managing patient records, handling billing and insurance matters, and even some elements of patient care, such as cleanings and preliminary examinations.

As a dentist, your role isn't to micromanage these tasks but to empower your staff to carry them out effectively. Trust in the competence and skills of your team, provide them with the appropriate training, and give them the autonomy they need to excel in their roles. This not only increases office efficiency but also creates an environment where everyone feels valued and motivated.

No matter how adept you may be as a dentist, your talent and expertise alone cannot guarantee the success and growth of your practice. If your team is unmotivated, lacks harmony, and exhibits poor performance and service, these are barriers to your success. It's akin to having a well-oiled, high-powered engine (you, the dentist) trying to drive a vehicle with flat tires (a subpar team). The engine's potential is wasted because the tires are not equipped to handle the power and speed. Similarly, without a proficient and dedicated team, your skills as a top-notch dentist are underutilized, and your practice's success will indeed be limited.

There are numerous tasks that can, and should, be delegated to your team to ensure smooth operations and effective management. For example, administrative tasks, such as scheduling appointments, communicating with patients, handling billing, and managing patient records, can be delegated to your front office team. Your dental assistants and hygienists can take on responsibilities like preliminary examinations, dental prophylaxis, and preparing patients for procedures.

Marketing and social media management can be handed over to a dedicated team member. By moving these tasks off of our plate, you're able to focus on your primary role: providing dental care. Remember that we make money when our handpieces are being used, not sitting in the sterilization bag.

C. Building a Great Dental Team: A Concise Guide

1. Recruit Skillfully

When looking for candidates, it is crucial to identify individuals who not only possess the necessary technical skills for the job but also exhibit traits that contribute to a positive work environment. These traits include effective communication, strong teamwork capabilities, and the ability to adapt to changing circumstances.

Finding the right team member can be one of the greatest challenges in your office. It requires a thorough search and evaluation process to identify individuals who possess the necessary skills, experience, and cultural fit. While many hardworking people are already employed, there will be unsuccessful individuals who are looking for work. These employees are not suitable for hiring, as they may potentially disrupt your office environment and have a tendency to leave within a relatively short period (12-18 months). All the training and effort will be wasted.

Continue searching, as there will be moments when exceptional employees are actively seeking job opportunities. Perhaps they have relocated to the area or their previous workplace has been acquired by corporate dentistry, causing great staff to flee. It could also be that they were previously stay-at-home parent and now that their children are older, they are ready to reenter the workforce.

I know from experience that when there is a sudden shortage of employees, we feel the need to fill the spot asap. Imagine if you lost all of your front office within a month due to maternity leave, moving out of town, going to college, or something else. You would need to hire someone fast to fill the opening or else you would be in trouble.

Let me share with you one incident when I hired an assistant too quickly and paid the price later on. At one time, my practice was extremely short staffed, so we ended up hiring an experienced assistant. Little did we know, she came with a crazy boyfriend, and she was an alcoholic. I helped her out many times by giving her money to repair her car. Meanwhile, her crazy boyfriend, who was into knives, would show up at work with them. He wanted to show off his home made knives.

After enough complaints about the crazy knife guy from my team, we decided that it was best that she went somewhere else. We terminated her position, but the story did not end there. One night, her boyfriend followed me home and discovered where I lived. Then, he came on another night and slashed my tires along with running his knife all around my car. I called the cops, but there were no cameras; thus, nothing was done. The car had to be towed to the body shop and it took them one month to finish the work. I felt sorry for the girl, who had to deal with this crazy person.

2. TRAIN EFFECTIVELY

This is one area in which small dental offices often lack. It's not that they don't want to offer effective training; it's that they don't have the resources to do so. One of my cousins started working as a nurse, and his training program was 6 months. Usually, when we hire someone, we throw them in the office to fend for themselves.

Nevertheless, once you have hired your team, it is important to invest in their ongoing professional development. Do you have a training program, or do you let whoever is already there to train the new staff? Regular training sessions provide an opportunity to enhance your staff's skills, expand their knowledge base, and sharpen their expertise. This not only boosts their confidence but also fosters a culture of continuous learning within the organization.

3. FOSTER A POSITIVE CULTURE

In order to create a thriving work environment, it is crucial to cultivate a positive, team-oriented culture. Encourage mutual respect and collaboration, promoting a sense of unity and shared purpose. It is equally important to ensure that each team member feels valued and recognized for their unique contributions, which further strengthens the positive culture within the organization. Some Doctors complain that they can never get any good employees. They are half right because that story is one-sided.

Unfortunately, some office environments are toxic pits. No matter how amazing your new hire may be, they can be influenced by the negativity around them. It's like placing one good apple with a bunch of bad apples: eventually, the good apple will be affected. The importance of fostering a positive and supportive workplace culture cannot be stressed enough. Even if you find a great new team member, they will turn bad quickly when added to an already toxic environment. Thus, it's important to clean house first before adding great team members.

4. COMMUNICATE OPENLY

Communication is key to fostering a collaborative and productive work environment. It is important to ensure that every team member is fully aware of the office's goals and objectives, as well as their individual roles and responsibilities in achieving them. Encourage open dialogue, welcome feedback, and be receptive to discussions that can lead to innovative ideas and solutions. Transparent and open communication allows the team to thrive and work towards shared success.

5. Motivate and Reward

One of the most effective ways to keep your team motivated is by acknowledging and appreciating their hard work. Incentives, rewards, or even simple words of appreciation can go a long way in boosting morale and productivity. When team members feel recognized and valued for their contributions, it creates a positive work environment that fosters even greater dedication and commitment.

So, take the time to say thank you and show your team that their efforts are truly valued. The impact of a simple thank you can be immeasurable and have a lasting effect on team morale and performance.

While cash bonuses can certainly be an exciting motivator for your team, they are not the only or the most effective method of motivation. Recognition of a job well done, opportunities for professional growth, and a supportive work environment can often be more motivating. A workplace culture that appreciates and acknowledges the hard work of its employees, irrespective of their role or position, can significantly boost morale and commitment. The key is to understand what truly drives your team and to provide rewards that resonate on a deeper, more personal level.

What do you do for team members who have been with you for 2, 5, 7, 10 years, or more? Do you go about your day, or do you do anything to celebrate them? They remember and know how many years they have been with you and so should you. Every business is looking for amazing team members, and if you have one, show that you appreciate them by giving them a plaque or some another business will steal them.

Presenting a plaque to a team member who has served for many years is a powerful affirmation of their contribution to your dental practice. This expression of gratitude commemorates their years of service and also their value within the team. This recognition not only boosts the individual's morale and motivation but also sets a positive example for other team members. It encourages a culture of loyalty and commitment, which are key attributes for the success of any leader, particularly in a dental office setting. Sadly, few dental offices do this for their team.

I recommend giving plaques for years served at year 2,5,7,10, and beyond. Order 2 plaques, one for them to take home and another for the office. Keeping one in the office does 2 things. One, it allows other team members to see this daily and reminds them that the boss is good. Second, it shows patients that the team members are appreciated and wanted. Plan on spending $300-$500 for each occasion. If you complain that that is too pricey, then I have a question for you: How much stress and cost is involved in finding another team member and training them to become proficient in your office?

D. Identify and Focus on Each Person's Skills and Potential

To identify these skills, you may utilize performance reviews, one-on-one discussions, or even skills assessment tools. Encourage your team to share their interests and areas of expertise. This not only promotes a culture of openness but also helps in the identification of untapped potential. Some like back office and others like front office duties, while there may be few who hate answering the phones.

Once these skills are identified, focus on nurturing them through targeted training and development programs. Empower your team by providing opportunities for growth and challenging them to take on tasks that will utilize and further develop their skills. Encourage employees to utilize their talents in problem-solving, decision-making, and creative thinking.

Implement a system that encourages innovative ideas, allowing individuals to contribute in ways that align with their unique abilities. Regular talent audits can also be a beneficial practice, enabling you to keep track of evolving skills and talents within your team.

E. Guiding Towards Self-Improvement

Leaders cannot mandate improvement; they can only foster an environment conducive to growth and provide guidance. Each team member must take personal initiative in order to grow their skills and overcome challenges. You can provide all the resources, training, and advice in the world, but without individual motivation and commitment to self-improvement, real change will not occur.

Inspiring this drive for self-improvement starts with creating an atmosphere of mutual respect and open communication, where each team member feels valued and heard. Encourage them to take ownership of their roles, set personal goals, and strive for excellence in their respective tasks within the dental practice. When they make mistakes, don't scold them. Acknowledge that a mistake was committed and move on.

F. Stop Micromanagement

Dentists are often micromanagers, an attribute nurtured during their time in dental school. The precision demanded in dental procedures requires keen attention to detail, a quality that naturally translates into their leadership style. However, it may not produce the same results when applied to a team or a business. Micromanaging may limit the autonomy and creative freedom of your team members, potentially stifling innovation and growth within your dental practice. Strike a balance between providing guidance and allowing your team the freedom to develop their own problem-solving strategies and ideas.

A common misconception among leaders in the dental field is the belief that controlling all aspects of the operation will minimize errors. This belief stems from the fear of mistakes, which are often viewed as setbacks rather than opportunities for learning and growth.

Although this control can lead to consistency in quality, it can also create an environment of dependency, where team members feel their input is not valued or trusted. This can hinder their professional development viewpoints and creative problem-solving skills. In this type of office, 80-90% of the non-dental duties will be done by the dentist.

SUMMARY

Creating an exceptional team in a dental practice involves more than just hiring skilled professionals. It requires a leadership style that fosters respect, open communication, and personal growth. Dentists must resist the urge to micromanage and, instead, strive to strike a balance between providing guidance and promoting autonomy. Leaders must view mistakes not as setbacks but as opportunities for learning and growth.

The next chapter might be the hardest thing to do: let go and allow someone else to handle the challenge.

CHAPTER 6:

More Freedom: The Power of Delegation

As Ronald Reagan once wisely said: "Surround yourself with the best people you can find, delegate authority, and don't interfere as long as the policy you've decided upon is being carried out."

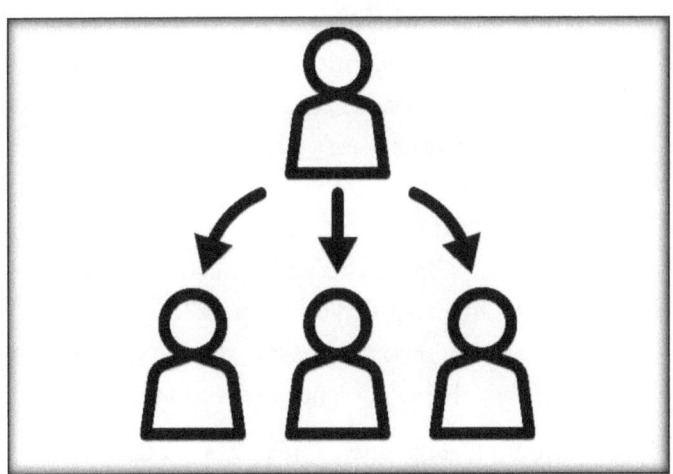

Learning Objectives

A. Take charge
B. Some tasks cannot be delegated
C. Stay calm because your team notices
D. More free time
E. The process of delegation
F. Failures and setbacks
G. Pick the right person for the task

A. Take Charge

Taking charge of the situation doesn't mean micromanaging every single task. It entails stepping back, trusting your team, and allowing them to excel in their roles. You assume the role of a conductor, orchestrating the symphony of tasks required to keep the dental office running smoothly, while not diving in to play each instrument yourself.

Consider a situation where a sudden influx of patients puts your practice into a busy, chaotic state. As a leader, you take a moment, assess the situation, and start delegating tasks based on your understanding of your team's strengths. You ask your most seasoned dental assistant to handle the complex cases, while the receptionist is entrusted with efficiently managing patient intake and scheduling. The billing specialist is tasked with ensuring that all of the patients' financial details are handled accurately. You don't hover over them, second-guessing their decisions, but you make yourself available for guidance and support.

Open communication and feedback are crucial. Regularly check in with your team to ensure everything is moving along as planned, and intervene only when necessary. Ask for updates not to micromanage, but to stay informed and provide assistance if needed.

In the end, the day is a success—not because you managed every little detail, but because you effectively directed your team, enabling them to leverage their skills and expertise. This is a prime example of leadership in a dental office setting: a balance of clear direction, delegation, and trust, without micromanaging.

B. SOME TASKS CANNOT BE DELEGATED

There are certain tasks that a dentist cannot delegate, as they are legally bound by the dental board regulations. These responsibilities typically involve clinical dentistry and direct patient care that requires the dentist's expertise and training. Examples include diagnosing dental disease, creating treatment plans, performing surgical procedures, and other complex interventions. These aspects of your practice demand your direct involvement and cannot be handed over, ensuring the highest standards of patient safety and care. You have plenty of things to do, so stop micromanaging your team (if you are a micromanager).

Years ago, when I was working as an associate for other dentists, I spent only three days at one particular office. This office had multiple associates working during the week, while the owner dentist was absent from that location. The office seemed to be stuck in the 1950s, despite it being 2005. There was an incident that caught my attention and ultimately led to my resignation. During a crown seat appointment, I noticed that the temporary crown had been cemented with a permanent cement. I had to remove it in order to proceed.

However, when the new crown didn't fit properly, I informed the office manager that it needed to be re-prepped and sent back to the lab. To my surprise, she insisted that it had to be cemented that day. I expressed my inability to do so, but she took matters into her own hands and cemented the crown herself.

Legally, she was not authorized to perform such a procedure, but she did it anyway. It seemed like she and the owner dentists were accustomed to engaging in questionable practices in that office. That incident marked my last day at that place. Unfortunately, similar dental offices with questionable practices exist out there.

In most cases, engaging in unauthorized tasks within a dental office may not immediately attract the attention of the authorities. This includes instances where unlicensed team members perform duties that legally require a license. However, if the dental board discovers such malpractices, the consequences can be severe. Not only may hefty fines be imposed, but the dental license could also be temporarily or even permanently suspended in extreme cases. This is a risk that should not be taken lightly, as the loss of a license can have irreversible consequences on one's career and reputation in the healthcare field.

Whistleblowing on businesses has become easier nowadays compared to the past. A few years ago, I had to terminate an employee who was deeply upset and sought revenge by attempting to harm my business. Among his actions was filing false claims with the dental board against my dental office. Consequently, an investigator paid us a visit. During their inspection, we couldn't conceal anything, as they were trained to interrogate all team members, verify licenses, and more. Two weeks later, we received a clean bill of health for my office. This outcome demonstrates that if any illicit activities were taking place, they would have been discovered, and I would have faced penalties.

C. Stay Calm Because Your Team Notices

We know the old saying, "monkey see money do" and this applies to our office. When a dental procedure takes an unforeseen turn, it's your leadership readiness that comes into play. You must maintain a level-headed demeanor, reassuring both your patient and your team. You calmly reassess the situation, consider the available options, and decide on a new course of action. This might mean altering the treatment plan, referring the patient out, or even rescheduling the procedure.

When your staff observes you handling high-pressure situations with a calm demeanor, it instills in them a deeper faith in your capabilities. This calmness under pressure assures them that you are in control and capable of navigating the team through any challenges that arise. Your ability to remain calm, composed, and decisive in the most stressful situations is a powerful testament to your leadership, boosting the team's confidence in your guidance and strengthening the overall success of your dental practice.

D. More Free Time

Having more free time as a result of effective delegation can open up a world of possibilities, enriching both your professional and personal life. On a professional level, you can use the additional time to see more patients, thus increasing office revenue. You could choose to focus on more complex dental cases, which will increase office revenue. The freedom from routine tasks gives you the opportunity to work less, enabling a healthier work-life balance, which is critical for long-term success and wellbeing.

On a personal level, this newfound time can be invested in strengthening your relationships with family and friends or even pursuing hobbies and travels that enrich your life outside the dental office. The gift of time from effective delegation and leadership can be leveraged to enhance every aspect of your life, driving success not just in your dental practice but also in your personal satisfaction and happiness.

Jeff Bezos, founder of Amazon, is an excellent case study in effective leadership and delegation. No leader single-handedly can manage every single aspect of a vast corporation like Amazon. The complexity and sheer size of operations necessitate delegation. Bezos is known for building a strong leadership team, known as the "S-team," responsible for various aspects of Amazon's operations.

He empowered these leaders to make decisions and act effectively within their areas of expertise, which in turn has been instrumental in fueling Amazon's growth and success. This approach is a testament to his understanding of leadership: knowing when to delegate, whom to delegate to, and how to create an environment that encourages innovation and responsibility.

E. The Process of Delegation

1. First, **identify the tasks** that can be delegated. These are often routine tasks or those that don't necessarily require your expertise.

2. Next, **select the right people** to delegate these tasks to. Choose individuals who have the necessary skills and a reliable track record.

3. Third, **clearly communicate your expectations**. Ensure that the person understands the task, the outcome you expect, and the deadline.

4. The fourth step is **providing the necessary resources and authority**. The delegate should have the tools, information, and power they need to complete the task.

5. Next, **monitor progress and provide feedback**. Don't micromanage, but do make sure the delegate knows they can come to you with any issues or questions.

6. Lastly, **reward and recognize good work**. Positive reinforcement fosters a culture of continuous learning and improvement and will motivate your team to take on more tasks.

Delegation is a skill that develops with practice. It might feel uncomfortable at first, especially if you are a micromanager, but as you allow it more and more and see the see the benefits, you will become more comfortable with it.

F. Failures and Setbacks

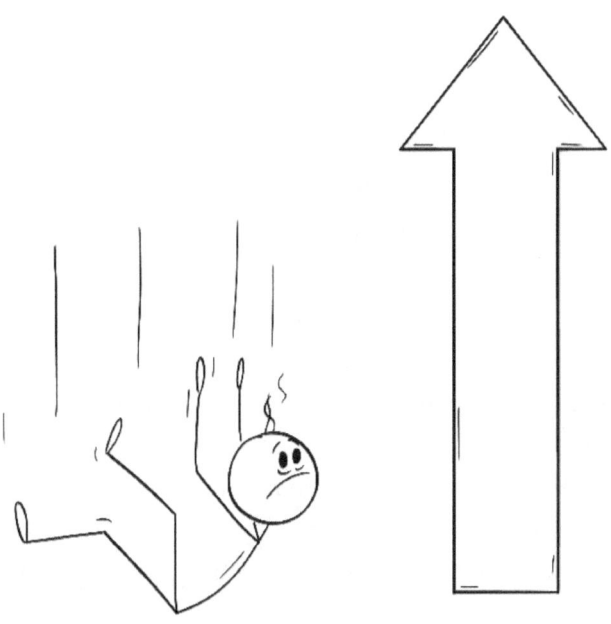

In cases where an employee doesn't succeed in a task, it's crucial to encourage them to try again. This process is an opportunity for learning and improvement. Your role here is not to penalize failure, but to frame it as a stepping stone towards success. Provide constructive feedback highlighting areas for improvement, and offer guidance on how to approach the task differently. Reiterate your confidence in their abilities, and remind them that everyone encounters setbacks on the road to success.

Sometimes, having a fresh pair of eyes to take a look at situation can help. One person may see it one way and cannot overcome the barrier, but two people working on the same project will definitely see more than one possibility.

When we were searching for new team members, I entrusted the task to my two most experienced team members in the office. They diligently scouted for candidates, but after about two weeks, they found themselves facing a difficult decision. They identified three exceptional team players, but, unfortunately, we only had two positions available.

The choice became arduous. To resolve this, we convened a meeting around a whiteboard. I requested clarification on the job requirements and the desired qualities of the ideal candidate. Since we weren't specifically seeking highly experienced individuals, as we already had two, and having more than one experienced individuals in the same department might lead to conflicts, a decision was eventually reached. After a thorough discussion that lasted approximately ten minutes, they reached a conclusion on their own. Sometimes, discussing matters out loud with others proves beneficial, yielding a satisfactory outcome.

G. Pick the Right Person for the Task

Not all tasks are suited to all employees, and it's essential to have a clear understanding of your team's strengths, weaknesses, and areas of expertise. When delegating tasks, consider the nature of the work and the skills it requires. Then, match this to the individual who is most equipped to take it on.

This is not just about their technical abilities, but also their passion and interest in the task at hand. The right person for a task is someone who has the necessary skills, but also the enthusiasm to see it through to completion. Assigning the right tasks to the right people is a surefire way to promote efficiency, job satisfaction, and, ultimately, the success of your dental practice.

Recognizing that people function at different speeds is also a pivotal aspect of leadership. Some team members may excel in fast-paced environments, swiftly completing tasks with efficiency and precision. Others might thrive at a slower pace, taking their time to meticulously execute tasks and ensuring every detail is attended to. A task with a tight deadline might be better suited for the swift executer, while a task requiring a meticulous approach may be ideal for the methodical worker.

When we assign a high priority task to someone who has a low probability of finishing it successfully, we are essentially setting that person up for failure. This can be demoralizing and can hinder their overall productivity and motivation.

Summary

Effective delegation is a vital leadership skill that promotes efficiency in a dental practice. It involves identifying the strengths, weaknesses, and interests of your team members and assigning tasks that align with these characteristics. People operate at different speeds; some excel in fast-paced environments, while others work best at a slower pace with a focus on detail. Assigning tasks appropriately contributes to the success of a dental practice, avoids setting team members up for failure, and fosters a positive and productive work environment.

CHAPTER 7:

How to Make Changes in the Office

"The only constant in life is change."
Greek philosopher Heraclitus

LEARNING OBJECTIVES

A. The need for change
B. Steps for successful changes
C. Other matters to keep in mind

A. THE NEED FOR CHANGE

It's often said that the only constant in life is change. Yet, it's undeniable that change can be unsettling, primarily because its ushers in the unknown. Human beings are creatures of habit, finding comfort and safety in familiarity. When introduced to changes, especially those that might alter our established routines or ways of working, fear and resistance can creep in. This fear is often not about the change itself but, rather, about the uncertainty that accompanies it. Staff members might fear that they won't be able to master a new process, or they might worry about how it will impact their roles.

Expanding the team with new members, introducing new hours of operation, implementing new dental procedures, or otherwise diving into an unknown territory can make the team anxious. We have brought many new changes to my office, and while a new procedure may seem fairly straightforward, in reality, there will be lots of unknowns. One such example was a case of traditional braces.

We put braces on a child who did not have the best mom. The child was 12 with a severe class 3 molar relationship. We needed to see him every month or else he would have needed surgery. The child's teeth were not the mom's priority. She brought him in once in 4 months and had all kinds of excuses. The payment for the case was made by the grandma, not the mom.

After 12 months of getting nowhere with this patient, we refunded the money and referred the patient to an orthodontist. Plus, I informed the orthodontist about the challenges that we faced with the patient. We did not expect such occurrences when we were gearing up to perform orthodontics, so this lesson was learned with some stress.

To successfully execute the desired change, it is crucial to develop a comprehensive action plan that outlines the specific steps for implementation, a well-defined timeline, and the necessary resources required for each phase. This detailed plan will provide a clear roadmap, ensuring a smooth and efficient transition towards achieving the desired outcome.

Without a well-defined plan for change, plans can go the wrong way. Several years ago, we implemented dental implants with bone grafts. I encountered a patient who required extraction, implant placement, and a bone graft on tooth 5. It was an ideal case, and I was brimming with excitement. Having completed numerous implant courses, I felt ready to tackle this challenge.

I developed a treatment plan and handed it over to my front office staff. However, to my dismay, they struggled to explain the purpose of a bone graft to the patient. I quickly realized that the fault lay with me; I had neglected to sit down with my team beforehand and provide them with a comprehensive explanation. Despite the team's difficulties, we managed to satisfy the patient in the end. Had the patient not been content, we would have risked losing the case.

B. Steps for Successful Change

1. Identify the Need for Change, the "Why:" Before implementing anything new, it is crucial to thoroughly comprehend the underlying reasons for its necessity. This may include adding new procedures like traditional braces or dental implant placement, streamlining operations to optimize efficiency and resource allocation, or other needed changes. "Why" do we need to make this change.

Let's use an example to demonstrate how to incorporate change easier: A must-have technology for every dental office is the Motorola CLP 1040 walkie talkie. (Newer models may be out) These devices greatly enhance communication efficiency within the office, allowing for swift and seamless interaction among the staff. With walkie talkies, the dental team can easily coordinate patient appointments, share important updates, and respond promptly to emergencies. This answers the Why.

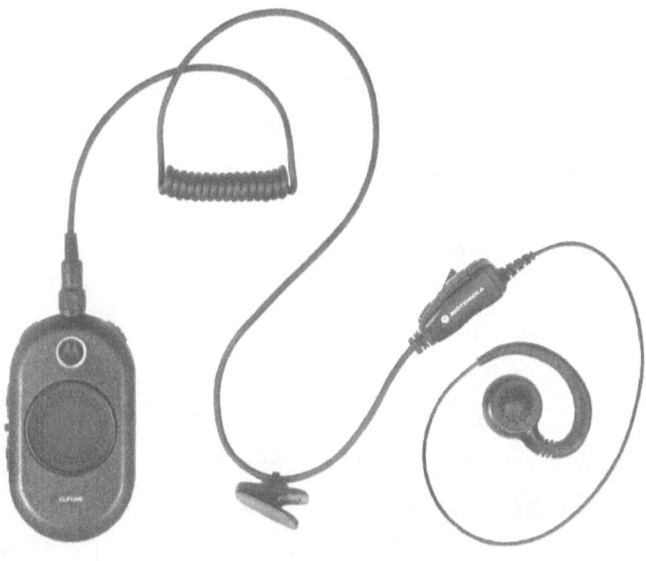

2. Plan for the Change: Lay the groundwork for a solid and well-executed transformation. This includes identifying key milestones, allocating resources, engaging stakeholders (for large corporate offices), and establishing a clear timeline.

The plan would be how to incorporate these units into their daily work life. Motorola CLP1040 walkie talkies have 2 parts: the earpiece and the actual unit. The unit has a clip for belts or if the team member does not wear a belt, it can fit into a pocket of their clothing. The earpieces come in many different sizes, and they are specific to each team member.

3. Identify Your Potential Obstacles: Change is rarely a smooth journey. Try to identify potential obstacles upfront. These obstacles may range from resistance to change within your team to lack of necessary resources or even regulatory complexities.

One obstacle for the walkie talkie is earpiece and at times, it can be very challenging. This part fits into the ear and has a cord but this cord can get caught or tangled on things. Furthermore, this can be distracting because of the device in one ear, and we still need to communicate and listen with the other ear. At times it feels like two different people are talking to each of our ears at the same time. This may hinder their daily routine because while talking with a patient or on the phone, a team member can talk into the walkie talkie, and confusion can arise when 2 or more people are talking at the same time.

4. Communicate with Your Team: Take the time to have open and honest discussions with your team, providing thorough explanations of the proposed change will help the process. Clearly articulate the reasons behind the change, and, more importantly, outline the specific benefits and positive outcomes it will bring. You can effectively engage your team and cultivate a shared understanding and commitment towards embracing the change.

Even with comprehensive knowledge and thorough preparation, the path to implementing a change is rarely smooth. Unforeseen challenges and obstacles inevitably arise, serving as barriers to progress. These unforeseen circumstances might stem from various sources, and their nature might be entirely unexpected.

5. Addressing Resistance to Change: There will always be individuals who are resistant to change, no matter the benefits it may bring. This resistance can stem from fear of the unknown, concern over job security, or simply a reluctance to alter established routines.

Despite all efforts to communicate the necessity for change, some may remain steadfast in their resistance. In such cases, it may be necessary to make tough decisions for the overall success of your dental practice. If an individual's resistance to change hinders the progress and harmony of the team, and after exhausting all solutions to address their concerns, it might be in the best interest of the practice to consider their removal. Decisions like these aren't easy, but they're sometimes necessary for the long-term health and success of your dental office.

6. Provide Training: Offer comprehensive training and ongoing support to staff members to effectively adapt to the new change. This includes providing them with the necessary resources, guidance, and mentorship to enhance their skills and knowledge.

We set aside 1 hour so the team could practice and become familiar with the technology. We also did mock drills. After that time period, everyone became familiar with the walkie talkie.

7. Monitor Progress: Consistently review the progress of the change in order to make any necessary adjustments. This ensures that the change is effectively integrated into the day-to-day operations of the office, promoting a smooth transition and maximizing its impact.

In the first week with the walkie talkies, we reviewed our progress daily and made adjustments for how to operate the system better.

8. Review and Refine: Once the change has been implemented, consistently review its effectiveness. Seek feedback from your team to gain valuable insights. Take the necessary steps to make refinements and adjustments, ensuring that the change is working optimally and aligning with the unique needs of your practice.

To successfully implement a change, it is crucial to diligently roll it out in accordance with the training plan. This involves ensuring that all team members are well taught about the new equipment/process. This way, they are informed about their respective roles and responsibilities, fostering a clear understanding of the expectations and objectives.

Providing this additional level of detail and clarity, we can enhance the likelihood of a smooth and effective implementation.

C. Other Matters to Keep in Mind

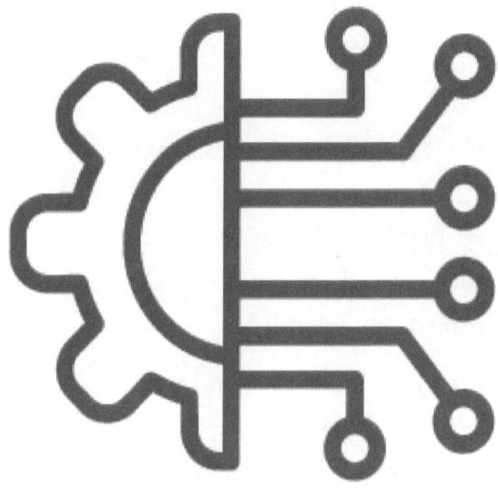

1. Align Change with Your Office Vision: Any change you implement should align with the broader vision for your dental office. This includes your goals, values, and the culture you've cultivated within your team. These changes are more likely to be accepted and embraced by your staff, leading to a more successful implementation. Your vision should guide all of your actions and decisions, serving as a compass during times of change.

2. Invest in Growth: If you have plans to expand and grow your dental office, it's essential to invest in technology. Innovative tools and equipment enhance the overall patient experience while also improving your team's efficiency and productivity. However, this doesn't mean you should purchase every new gadget or software that comes onto the market.

Instead, selectively invest in technology that aligns with your office's growth strategy and that your team has the capacity to use it effectively. In my experience, 80% of new technology or equipment is not worth its value. One test that we perform to determine if something is worth the value is called the eBay test.

The eBay test involves examining the resale value of dental equipment after one, three, and five years. Let's consider the example of Cerec. A brand-new unit costs approximately $150,000, whereas a five-year-old unit sells for $25,000 or less. Why does the value drop so significantly?

There are numerous theories on this, and we had our own experience for a brief period. In our office, we found that we could only use it for about 80% of our preparations. Scanning was more cumbersome compared to traditional impressions, and the crown fabrication process took a considerable amount of time.

Additionally, we encountered difficulties in milling for Zirconia crowns without increasing office time. (We can mill Zirconia crowns, but since it's harder and takes more time, the process eats up more of the milling burs) The machine required regular servicing, and the burs needed frequent replacement.

To achieve a perfect match for all teeth colors, we would have had to expand our inventory of tooth blocks, resulting in increased costs. One staff member in our office assumed the role of a lab technician and took on the responsibility of designing and glazing the crown before placing it in the oven.

Although there were more steps involved, the bottom line was that I could spend just 30 minutes on a preparation and send it to the lab for an excellent Zirconia crown. Because of the sheer volume of the crowns that laboratories complete, they have hundreds of shades, and they can fix little issues that would take much longer time to fix in our office. This approach proved to be much simpler for me. However, if you are currently using Cerec and find it to be a valuable tool, that's fantastic and an excellent example of how every dentist's practice is unique.

SUMMARY

Change in any dental practice is inevitable and often necessary for growth and improvement. This could involve the adoption of new technologies or methods or even redefining roles within the office. Such transitions should be carefully managed, and every change doesn't guarantee improvement, but every improvement will indeed require a change.

CHAPTER 8:

Summary

Learning to lead involves understanding each team member's role, strengths, and areas for improvement. This understanding allows for clear communication of expectations, reducing ambiguity and the stress that comes with it. Moreover, a good leader facilitates open communication, encourages feedback, and values team input. This promotes a collaborative culture where everyone feels heard and valued.

Leadership also involves setting a positive example by demonstrating respect, empathy, and integrity, which will foster the same qualities within the team. By showing dedication to continual learning and improvement, a leader will inspire their team to strive for the same.

A leader must be proactive in recognizing and addressing issues before they escalate. This requires an ability to make difficult decisions, provide constructive feedback, and, when necessary, enforce consequences for poor performance.

Learning to lead is about fostering a positive, communicative, and productive work environment. By mastering these skills, a dentist can transform their office from a place of chaos and stress to a thriving, successful dental practice. This is why developing leadership skills is not just an aspiration, but a critical prerequisite for success in today's world.

Each individual harbors their own set of beliefs and qualities that shape their behavior and actions. These are the core principles that guide us, influencing our decisions, our responses to challenges, and even our interactions with others. Understanding and harnessing these traits can significantly enhance your effectiveness as a leader.

A great leader recognizes their unique qualities and leverages them to inspire their team, foster a positive work environment, and ultimately drive the success of their dental practice.

A leader's influence is profound and far-reaching, significantly affecting the dynamics within a dental office. A competent leader cultivates an environment of reassurance, respect, and recognition that motivates employees to strive for excellence. They inspire others not merely through words but through actions, setting high standards and leading by example. Their optimism, resilience, and commitment in the face of challenges can ignite the same qualities in their team members, fostering a culture of perseverance and solution-oriented thinking.

Great leaders acknowledge and appreciate the efforts of their team, creating a sense of belonging and encouraging continued dedication and productivity. Successful leadership in a dental office is synonymous with promoting a culture of mutual respect, continuous learning, and unwavering commitment to great things.

I hope that you found this book interesting and that the ideas that I have presented are worthy of your time. No matter where you are in the leadership scale (more or less skilled), know that it takes time to become an effective leader. Moreover, the learning process of a leader never stops. We are exposed to new challenges constantly, and each time we overcome one, we learn and become stronger. I wish you great success with your dental office and to make it a great day!

Ike H. Rahimi, DMD

www.ingramcontent.com/pod-product-compliance
Lightning Source LLC
Chambersburg PA
CBHW031434210526
45464CB00005B/2194